I am so glad you are here! Before we begin this new session, I want to take the time and let you know that YOU have been prayed for! It is not a coincidence you are participating in this online Bible study.

My prayer for you this session is simple: **that you will grow closer to our Lord as you dig into His Word each and every day!** As you develop the discipline of being in God's Word on a daily basis, I pray you will fall in love with Him even more as you spend time reading from the Bible.

Each day before you read the assigned Scripture(s), pray and ask God to help you understand it. Invite Him to speak to you through His Word. Then listen. **It's His job to speak to you and your job to listen and obey.**

Take time to read the verses over and over again. We are told in Proverbs to *search and you will find.*

*"Search for it like silver, and hunt for it like hidden treasure. Then you will understand."*

We are thrilled to provide many different resources for you as you participate in our online Bible study:

- <u>Names of God</u> Study Journal (print out or purchase online)
- Reading Plan
- Weekly Blog posts (Mondays, Wednesdays, & Fridays)
- Weekly Memory Verses
- Weekly Monday Videos
- Weekly Challenges
- Online community: Facebook, Twitter, Instagram, LoveGodGreatly.com
- Hashtags: #LoveGodGreatly #NamesofGod

All of us here at *Love God Greatly* can't wait to get started with you and hope to see you at the finish line. **Endure, persevere, press on – and don't give up!** Let's finish well what we are beginning today. We will be here every step of the way, *cheering you on!* **We are in this together.** Fight to rise early, to push back the stress of the day, to sit alone and spend time in God's Word! I can't wait to see what God has in store for us this session!

Journey with us as we learn to **Love God Greatly** with our lives!!!

# Table of Contents

# Our Community

*Love God Greatly* consists of a beautiful community of women who use a variety of technology platforms to keep each other accountable in God's Word.

*We start with a simple Bible reading plan, but it doesn't stop there.*

Some gather in homes and churches locally, while others connect online with women across the globe. Whatever the method, we lovingly lock arms and unite for this purpose…

*to Love God Greatly with our lives.*

In today's fast-paced technology driven world, it would be easy to study God's Word in an isolated environment that lacks encouragement or support, but that isn't the intention here at *Love God Greatly*. God created us to live in community with Him and with those around us.

*We need each other, and we live life better together.*

**Because of this, would you consider reaching out and studying with someone this session?**

**All of us have women in our lives who need friendship, accountability, and have the desire to dive into God's Word on a deeper level.** Rest assured we'll be studying right alongside you - learning with you, cheering for you, enjoying sweet fellowship, and smiling from ear to ear as we watch God unite women together - intentionally connecting hearts and minds for His glory.

**It's pretty unreal - this opportunity we have to not only grow closer to God through this study, but also to each other.**

So here's the challenge: call your mom, your sister, your grandma, the girl across the street or the college friend across the country. Grab a group of girls from your church or workplace, or meet in a coffee shop with friends you have always wished you knew better. Utilize the beauty of connecting online for inspiration and accountability, and take opportunities to meet in person when you can.

*Arm in arm and hand in hand,*
*let's do this thing… together.*

We're proud of you.

We *really* want you to know that.

**We're proud of you for making the commitment to be in God's Word**… to be reading it each day and applying it to YOUR life - the beautiful life our Lord has given YOU.

Each session we offer a study journal that goes along with the verses we are reading. This journal is designed to help you interact with God's Word and learn to dig deeper - encouraging you to slow down to *really reflect* on what God is saying to you that day.

**At *Love God Greatly*, we use the S.O.A.P. Bible study method. Before we begin, we'd like to take a moment to define this method and share WHY we recommend using it during your quiet time.**

## Why S.O.A.P. it?

It's one thing to simply read Scripture. But when you interact with it, intentionally slowing down to REALLY reflect on it, suddenly words start popping off the page. The SOAP method allows you to dig deeper into Scripture and see more than if you simply read the verses and then went on your merry way. We encourage you to take the time to S.O.A.P. through our Bible studies and see for yourself how much more you get out of your daily reading. You'll be amazed.

## What does S.O.A.P. mean?

**S**- The S stands for Scripture. Physically write out the verses. You'll be amazed at what God will reveal to you just by taking the time to slow down and write out what you are reading!

**O**- The O stands for Observation. What do you see in the verses that you're reading? Who is the intended audience? Is there a repetition of words? What words stand out to you?

**A**- The A stands for Application. This is when God's Word becomes personal. What is God saying to me today? How can I apply what I just read to my own personal life? What changes do I need to make? Is there action that I need to take?

**P**- And finally, P stands for Prayer. Pray God's Word back to Him. Spend time thanking Him. If He has revealed something to you during this time in His Word, pray about it. If He has revealed some sin that is in your life, confess. And remember, He loves you dearly.

**EXAMPLE: Read: Colossians 1:5-8**

**S**- The faith and love that spring from the hope that is stored up for you in heaven and that you have already heard about in the word of truth, the gospel that has come to you. All over the world this gospel is bearing fruit and growing, just as it has been doing among you since the day you heard it and understood God's grace in all its truth. You learned it from Epaphras, our dear fellow servant, who is a faithful minister of Christ on our behalf, and who also told us of your love in the Spirit.

**O-**
- When you combine faith and love, you get hope.
- We have to remember that our hope is in heaven… it is yet to come.
- The gospel is the Word of Truth.
- The gospel is continually bearing fruit and growing from the first day to the last.
- It just takes one person to change a whole community… Epaphras.

**A-** God used one man, Epaphras, to change a whole town! I was reminded that we are simply called to tell others about Christ -it's God's job to spread the gospel, to grow it, and have it bear fruit. I felt today's verses were almost directly spoken to LGG… *"all over the world this gospel is bearing fruit and growing, just as it has been doing among you since the day you heard it and understood God's grace in all its truth."* It's so fun when God's Word becomes so alive and encourages us in our current situation! My passionate desire is that all the women involved in this Bible study will understand God's grace and have a thirst for His Word. Moved by this quote from my Bible commentary: *"God's Word is not just for our information, it is for our transformation."*

**P-** Dear Lord, please help me to be an "Epaphras" - to tell others about You and then leave the results in Your loving hands. Please help me to understand and apply what I have read today to my life personally, thereby becoming more and more like You each and every day. Help me to live a life that bears the fruit of faith and love… anchoring my hope in heaven, not here on earth. Help me to remember that the BEST is yet to come!

———————————

**Remember, the most important ingredients in the S.O.A.P. method are YOUR interaction with God's Word and your APPLICATION of His Word to YOUR life.**

**Blessed is the man whose** *"delight is in the law of the Lord, and on his law he meditates day and night. He is like a tree planted by streams of water, which yields its fruit in season and whose leaf does not wither. Whatever he does prospers."* **~ Psalm 1:2-3**

# Soap Reading Plan

|  |  | **Read** | **SOAP** |
|---|---|---|---|
| **WEEK 1** | Monday | Genesis 22:9-14 | Genesis 22:13-14 |
|  | Tuesday | Philippians 4:10-20 | Philippians 4:19 |
|  | Wednesday | Ephesians 3:14-21 | Ephesians 3:20-21 |
|  | Thursday | Matthew 6:25-34 | Matthew 6:31-33 |
|  | Friday | 2 Peter 1:2-4 | 2 Peter 1:3-4 |
|  | Response Day |  |  |
|  |  |  |  |
| **WEEK 2** | Monday | Psalm 23 | Psalm 23:1-3 |
|  | Tuesday | John 10:1-6; 11-15 | John 10:14-15 |
|  | Wednesday | Isaiah 40:11 | Isaiah 40:11 |
|  | Thursday | Luke 15:1-7 | Luke 15:7 |
|  | Friday | Psalm 100 | Psalm 100:3 |
|  | Response Day |  |  |
|  |  |  |  |
| **WEEK 3** | Monday | Luke 2:8-14 | Luke 2:13-14 |
|  | Tuesday | John 14:25-27 | John 14:27 |
|  | Wednesday | Philippians 4:6-7 | Philippians 4:7 |
|  | Thursday | Hebrews 13:20-21 | Hebrews 13:20 |
|  | Friday | John 16:31-33 | John 16:33 |
|  | Response Day |  |  |
|  |  |  |  |
| **WEEK 4** | Monday | Isaiah 28:29 | Isaiah 28:29 |
|  | Tuesday | Colossians 2:1-3 | Colossians 2:3 |
|  | Wednesday | James 1:1-7 | James 1:5-6 |
|  | Thursday | Revelation 7:11-12 | Revelation 7:11-12 |
|  | Friday | Isaiah 9:6-7 | Isaiah 9:6 |
|  | Response Day |  |  |
|  |  |  |  |
| **WEEK 5** | Monday | Matthew 1:18-23 | Matthew 1:23 |
|  | Tuesday | Isaiah 41:10 | Isaiah 41:10 |
|  | Wednesday | Matthew 28:16-20 | Matthew 28:20 |
|  | Thursday | Jeremiah 23:23-24 | Jeremiah 23:23-24 |
|  | Friday | Galatians 2:20 | Galatians 2:20 |
|  | Response Day |  |  |
|  |  |  |  |
| **WEEK 6** | Monday | Matthew 1:20-22 | Matthew 1:21 |
|  | Tuesday | Mark 2:16-17 | Mark 2:17 |
|  | Wednesday | 1 Timothy 1:15-17 | 1 Timothy 1:15 |
|  | Thursday | Isaiah 53:3-7 | Isaiah 53:6 |
|  | Friday | John 3:16-18 | John 3:16 |
|  | Response Day |  |  |

# Goals

We believe it's important to write out goals for each session. Take some time now and write three goals you would like to focus on this session as we begin to rise each day and dig into God's Word. Make sure and refer back to these goals throughout the next six weeks to help you stay focused. YOU CAN DO IT!!!

My goals for this session are:

1.


2.


3.


Signature:_____

Date:_____

# Intro into Names of God

What's In a Name?

In different cultures and in different times the naming of a baby is no small matter. Names were seriously considered, and then carefully chosen for a number of different reasons. Some named their children after their ancestors as a way of preserving a family's heritage. Others gave their children names that had special religious meaning. Some gave their children names with a meaning they hoped would come to characterize the child in his or her adulthood.

For example, one of my daughters is named Madeline Ember. Madeline comes from the name Mary Magdalene, the first person Jesus showed himself to after his resurrection. Ember is a small spark of fire. Through her name we wanted our Madeline to know that God values girls just as much as boys and we hope that in her heart her name would be a spark of faith that would grow to be a roaring fire of love for Christ.

Throughout Scripture we see parents give their children names that have some kind of meaning. Sometimes this meaning stems from something good (Hannah named her baby Samuel "… because I have asked him of the Lord." ~ 1 Sam. 1:20). Sometimes it is not so good (like when Eli's daughter-in-law found out that Eli and her husband had died and that the Ark of the Covenant had been captured, she named her baby Ichabod saying, "The glory has departed from Israel." ~ 1 Sam. 4).

Now when it comes to the names of God it is important to recognize that we do not name God.

## He names himself.

This is important because it shows that there is something specific he wants to reveal about himself in his names, which means we need to pay close attention.

He transcends time and space. We are told in Isaiah 55:8 that his thoughts and his ways are not like ours. He is exalted above all things and is incomprehensible. And yet he has condescended to make himself known to us in ways that we can understand. He has given himself names to help us see his character. God's many beautiful names reveal something about who he is and why he functions the way he does.

This is theology--the study of God.

# *Intro into Names of God*

But theology does not end with us simply knowing more facts about God. Theology starts with truth, but this truth takes root in our hearts and then influences our actions.

*"Disregard the study of God, and you sentence yourself to stumble and blunder through life blindfolded, as it were, with no sense of direction and no understanding of what surrounds you. This way you can waste your life and lose your soul."*

*—J.I. Packer*

During this study we will be looking at six of the names God has given himself.

We will look at the truths these names reveal about God, and how this should practically impact our everyday decisions, emotions, and relationships.

Come join us as we get to know God more fully. He shows himself to us because of his great love for us and we, in turn, should love, worship and rest in Him.

"O Lord, our Lord, how majestic is your name in all the earth! You have set your glory above the heavens."

— Psalm 8:1

**Week 1 Challenge** (Note: You can find this listed in our Monday blog post):

**Week 1 Memory Verse:**

His divine power has granted to us
*all things*
that pertain to
life and godliness,
*through the knowledge*
of him who called us to his own
glory and excellence,

2 PETER 1:3

LoveGodGreatly.com

# Week 1

**Prayer focus for this week:** Your Family

| | Praying | Praise |
|---|---|---|
| Monday | | |
| Tuesday | | |
| Wednesday | | |
| Thursday | | |
| Friday | | |

## SCRIPTURE FOR THIS WEEK

**Genesis 22:9-14 ESV**

⁹ When they came to the place of which God had told him, Abraham built the altar there and laid the wood in order and bound Isaac his son and laid him on the altar, on top of the wood. ¹⁰ Then Abraham reached out his hand and took the knife to slaughter his son. ¹¹ But the angel of the LORD called to him from heaven and said, "Abraham, Abraham!" And he said, "Here I am." ¹² He said, "Do not lay your hand on the boy or do anything to him, for now I know that you fear God, seeing you have not withheld your son, your only son, from me." ¹³ And Abraham lifted up his eyes and looked, and behold, behind him was a ram, caught in a thicket by his horns. And Abraham went and took the ram and offered it up as a burnt offering instead of his son. ¹⁴ So Abraham called the name of that place, "The LORD will provide"; as it is said to this day, "On the mount of the LORD it shall be provided."

**Philippians 4:10-20 ESV**

¹⁰ I rejoiced in the Lord greatly that now at length you have revived your concern for me. You were indeed concerned for me, but you had no opportunity. ¹¹ Not that I am speaking of being in need, for I have learned in whatever situation I am to be content. ¹² I know how to be brought low, and I know how to abound. In any and every circumstance, I have learned the secret of facing plenty and hunger, abundance and need. ¹³ I can do all things through him who strengthens me.

¹⁴ Yet it was kind of you to share my trouble. ¹⁵ And you Philippians yourselves know that in the beginning of the gospel, when I left Macedonia, no church entered into partnership with me in giving and receiving, except you only. ¹⁶ Even in Thessalonica you sent me help for my needs once and again. ¹⁷ Not that I seek the gift, but I seek the fruit that increases to your credit. ¹⁸ I have received full payment, and more. I am well supplied; having received from Epaphroditus the gifts you sent, a fragrant offering, a

sacrifice acceptable and pleasing to God. ¹⁹ And my God will supply every need of yours according to his riches in glory in Christ Jesus. ²⁰ To our God and Father be glory forever and ever. Amen.

**Ephesians 3:14-21 ESV**

¹⁴ For this reason I bow my knees before the Father, ¹⁵ from whom every family in heaven and on earth is named, ¹⁶ that according to the riches of his glory he may grant you to be strengthened with power through his Spirit in your inner being, ¹⁷ so that Christ may dwell in your hearts through faith—that you, being rooted and grounded in love,¹⁸ may have strength to comprehend with all the saints what is the breadth and length and height and depth, ¹⁹ and to know the love of Christ that surpasses knowledge, that you may be filled with all the fullness of God.

²⁰ Now to him who is able to do far more abundantly than all that we ask or think, according to the power at work within us, ²¹ to him be glory in the church and in Christ Jesus throughout all generations, forever and ever. Amen.

**Matthew 6:25-34 ESV**

²⁵ "Therefore I tell you, do not be anxious about your life, what you will eat or what you will drink, nor about your body, what you will put on. Is not life more than food, and the body more than clothing? ²⁶ Look at the birds of the air: they neither sow nor reap nor gather into barns, and yet your heavenly Father feeds them. Are you not of more value than they?²⁷ And which of you by being anxious can add a single hour to his span of life? ²⁸ And why are you anxious about clothing? Consider the lilies of the field, how they grow: they neither toil nor spin, ²⁹ yet I tell you, even Solomon in all his glory was not arrayed like one of these. ³⁰ But if God so clothes the grass of the field, which today is alive and tomorrow is thrown into the oven, will he not much more clothe you, O

you of little faith? [31] Therefore do not be anxious, saying, 'What shall we eat?' or 'What shall we drink?' or 'What shall we wear?' [32] For the Gentiles seek after all these things, and your heavenly Father knows that you need them all. [33] But seek first the kingdom of God and his righteousness, and all these things will be added to you.

[34] "Therefore do not be anxious about tomorrow, for tomorrow will be anxious for itself. Sufficient for the day is its own trouble.

**2 Peter 1:2-4 ESV**

[2] May grace and peace be multiplied to you in the knowledge of God and of Jesus our Lord. [3] His divine power has granted to us all things that pertain to life and godliness, through the knowledge of him who called us to his own glory and excellence, [4] by which he has granted to us his precious and very great promises, so that through them you may become partakers of the divine nature, having escaped from the corruption

that is in the world because of sinful desire.

# *Monday*

**Read:** Genesis 22:9-14

**Soap:** Genesis 22:13-14

**Scripture** — Write out the **Scripture** passage for the day.

**Observations** — Write down 1 or 2 **observations** from the passage.

# Monday

## Applications - Write down 1-2 **applications** from the passage.

## Pray - Write out a prayer over what you learned from today's passage.

-Visit our website today for the corresponding blog post!-

# Tuesday

**Read:** Philippians 4:10-20

**Soap:** Philippians 4:19

**Scripture** — Write out the **Scripture** passage for the day.

**Observations** — Write down 1 or 2 **observations** from the passage.

# Tuesday

*Applications* - Write down 1-2 **applications** from the passage.

*Pray* — Write out a prayer over what you learned from today's passage.

# Wednesday

**Read:** Ephesians 3:14-21

**Soap:** Ephesians 3:20-21

**Scripture**– Write out the **Scripture** passage for the day.

**Observations**– Write down 1 or 2 **observations** from the passage.

# Wednesday

*Applications* - Write down 1-2 **applications** from the passage.

*Pray* — Write out a prayer over what you learned from today's passage.

# Thursday

**Read:** Matthew 6:25-34

**Soap:** Matthew 6:31-33

**Scripture**— Write out the **Scripture** passage for the day.

**Observations**— Write down 1 or 2 **observations** from the passage.

# Thursday

*Applications* - Write down 1-2 **applications** from the passage.

*Pray* - Write out a prayer over what you learned from today's passage.

# Friday

**Read:** 2 Peter 1:2-4

**Soap:** 2 Peter 1:3-4

**Scripture**— Write out the **Scripture** passage for the day.

**Observations**— Write down 1 or 2 **observations** from the passage.

_Applications_ - Write down 1-2 **applications** from the passage.

_Pray_ — Write out a prayer over what you learned from today's passage.

-Visit our website today for the corresponding blog post!-

# Reflection Questions

## -JEHOVAH JIREH-

1. God provided Abraham "a ram in the thicket." Think about a time when God made a way to deliver you out of some difficult situation, stressful circumstance or overwhelming struggle. Reflect on those situations and circumstances and praise God now for the ways he provided and cared for you during those times.

2. Pray that God would show you a need in someone's life and that he would allow you to meet that need. Pray to be generous and sacrificial in your love and care of others. Praise God for the many ways he provides for your needs and ask Him to enable you to be sensitive and selfless to better meet the needs of others.

3. We are often willing to settle for "good" or "better," but God desires for us that which is "best." List the instances when God's provision for you was more abundant than you would have ever asked or imagined was even possible. Thank the Lord for his generosity and for the many ways he provides for your every need.

4. In what areas of your life are you particularly vulnerable to fear and worry? Confess your concerns to God and prayerfully ask him to help you seek his kingdom and his righteousness first and foremost in your life. Praise him for helping you to seek after the things of God before all else.

5. In what ways are you enslaved to sinful desires? Surrender these areas to Jesus and pray that God's Spirit will deliver you from these snares and free you to become a partaker of the divine nature. Give God the glory for your victories as you grow and mature in your faith.

# My Response

## -JEHOVAH JIREH-

**Week 2 Challenge** (Note: You can find this listed in our Monday blog post):

**Week 2 Memory Verse:**

Know that the Lord,
*he is God!*
It is he who made us,
and we are his;
*we are his people,*
and the sheep of his pasture.

PSALM 100:3

LoveGodGreatly.com

# Week 2

**Prayer focus for this week:** Your Country

| | Praying | Praise |
|---|---|---|
| Monday | | |
| Tuesday | | |
| Wednesday | | |
| Thursday | | |
| Friday | | |

**Psalm 23:1-3 ESV**

The LORD is my shepherd; I shall not want.

2 He makes me lie down in green pastures.

He leads me beside still waters.

3 He restores my soul.

He leads me in paths of righteousness

for his name's sake.

**John 10:1-6, 11-14 ESV**

"Truly, truly, I say to you, he who does not enter the sheepfold by the door but climbs in by another way, that man is a thief and a robber. 2 But he who enters by the door is the shepherd of the sheep. 3 To him the gatekeeper opens. The sheep hear his voice, and he calls his own sheep by name and leads them out. 4 When he has brought out all his own, he goes before them, and the sheep follow him, for they know his voice. 5 A stranger they will not follow, but they will flee from him, for they do not know the voice of strangers." 6 This figure of speech Jesus used with them, but they did not understand what he was saying to them.

11 I am the good shepherd. The good shepherd lays down his life for the sheep. 12 He who is a hired hand and not a shepherd, who does not own the sheep, sees the wolf coming and leaves the sheep and flees, and the wolf snatches them and scatters them. 13 He flees because he is a hired hand and cares nothing for the sheep. 14 I am the good shepherd. I know my own and my own know me,

**Isaiah 40:11 ESV**

[11] He will tend his flock like a shepherd; he will gather the lambs in his arms; he will carry them in his bosom, and gently lead those that are with young.

**Luke 15:1-7 ESV**

Now the tax collectors and sinners were all drawing near to hear him. [2] And the Pharisees and the scribes grumbled, saying, "This man receives sinners and eats with them."

[3] So he told them this parable: [4] "What man of you, having a hundred sheep, if he has lost one of them, does not leave the ninety-nine in the open country, and go after the one that is lost, until he finds it? [5] And when he has found it, he lays it on his shoulders, rejoicing. [6] And when he comes home, he calls together his friends and his neighbors, saying to them, 'Rejoice with me, for I have found my sheep that was lost.' [7] Just so, I tell you, there will be more joy in heaven over one sinner who repents than over ninety-nine righteous persons who need no repentance.

**Psalm 100 ESV**

Make a joyful noise to the LORD, all the earth!
[2]   Serve the LORD with gladness!
   Come into his presence with singing!
[3] Know that the LORD, he is God!
   It is he who made us, and we are his;
   we are his people, and the sheep of his pasture.
[4] Enter his gates with thanksgiving,
   and his courts with praise!
   Give thanks to him; bless his name!
[5] For the LORD is good;
   his steadfast love endures forever,
   and his faithfulness to all generations

# Monday

**Read:** Psalm 23

**Soap:** Psalm 23:1-3

**Scripture** — Write out the **Scripture** passage for the day.

**Observations** — Write down 1 or 2 **observations** from the passage.

# *Monday*

*Applications* - Write down 1-2 **applications** from the passage.

*Pray* - Write out a prayer over what you learned from today's passage.

# Tuesday

**Read:** John 10:1-6; 11-15

**Soap:** John 10:14-15

**Scripture**— Write out the **Scripture** passage for the day.

**Observations**— Write down 1 or 2 **observations** from the passage.

# Tuesday

*Applications* - Write down 1-2 **applications** from the passage.

*Pray* — Write out a prayer over what you learned from today's passage.

# Wednesday

**Read:** Isaiah 40:11

**Soap:** Isaiah 40:11

**Scripture** — Write out the **Scripture** passage for the day.

**Observations** — Write down 1 or 2 **observations** from the passage.

# Wednesday

*Applications* - Write down 1-2 **applications** from the passage.

*Pray* — Write out a prayer over what you learned from today's passage.

-Visit our website today for the corresponding blog post!--

# Thursday

**Read:** Luke 15:1-7

**Soap:** Luke 15:7

**Scripture** — Write out the **Scripture** passage for the day.

**Observations** — Write down 1 or 2 **observations** from the passage.

# Thursday

*Applications* – Write down 1-2 **applications** from the passage.

*Pray* – Write out a prayer over what you learned from today's passage.

# Friday

**Read:** Psalms 100

**Soap:** Psalms 100:3

**Scripture** — Write out the **Scripture** passage for the day.

**Observations** — Write down 1 or 2 **observations** from the passage.

# Friday

## Applications — Write down 1-2 **applications** from the passage.

## Pray — Write out a prayer over what you learned from today's passage.

-Visit our website today for the corresponding blog post!--

# Reflection Questions

## -JEHOVAH ROHI-

1. In what ways have you experienced the benefit of God's presence and care for you? Ask God to show you the many ways that he cares for you on a daily basis and praise him for his tender mercies toward you.

2. Are you more intimate with Jesus today than you were yesterday? If so, what has made this so? If not, what hinders you from enjoying a close, interpersonal relationship with the One who willingly laid down his life for you? Praise God for the way he loves you and ask Him to enable you to receive His divine love.

3. If the Good Shepherd provides food for his flock, are you feeding on God's Word or are you spiritually malnourished as a result of neglecting the Bible?

4. What has been your mindset about sharing your faith with another? Is there someone in your life that you'd like to speak with about Jesus but you have been hesitant to do so? Pray for the opportunity, the courage and the willingness to share God's truth with one who needs to hear about the gospel.

5. If God made us and we are his, how can our lives reflect the gratitude, devotion and honor that is due Him for his provision, nurturance and continued guidance? How does it make you feel to know that you are under God's watchful care? How will this truth change your attitude and actions when you are tempted to doubt his goodness and everlasting love and care for you?

# My Response

-WEEK 2-

**Week 3 Challenge** (Note: You can find this listed in our Monday blog post):

**Week 3 Memory Verse:**

Peace I leave with you;
*my peace I give to you.*
Not as the world gives do I give to you.
Let not your hearts be troubled,
*neither let them be afraid.*

JOHN 14:27

LoveGodGreatly.com

**Prayer focus for this week:** Your Friends

| | Praying | Praise |
|---|---|---|
| Monday | | |
| Tuesday | | |
| Wednesday | | |
| Thursday | | |
| Friday | | |

## SCRIPTURE FOR THIS WEEK

**Luke 2:8-14 ESV**

⁸ And in the same region there were shepherds out in the field, keeping watch over their flock by night. ⁹ And an angel of the Lord appeared to them, and the glory of the Lord shone around them, and they were filled with great fear. ¹⁰ And the angel said to them, "Fear not, for behold, I bring you good news of great joy that will be for all the people.¹¹ For unto you is born this day in the city of David a Savior, who is Christ the Lord. ¹² And this will be a sign for you: you will find a baby wrapped in swaddling cloths and lying in a manger." ¹³ And suddenly there was with the angel a multitude of the heavenly host praising God and saying,

¹⁴ "Glory to God in the highest,

and on earth peace among those with whom he is pleased!"

**John 14:25-27 ESV**

²⁵ "These things I have spoken to you while I am still with you. ²⁶ But the Helper, the Holy Spirit, whom the Father will send in my name, he will teach you all things and bring to your remembrance all that I have said to you. ²⁷ Peace I leave with you; my peace I give to you. Not as the world gives do I give to you. Let not your hearts be troubled, neither let them be afraid.

**Philippians 4:6-7 ESV**

⁶ do not be anxious about anything, but in everything by prayer and supplication with thanksgiving let your requests be made known to God. ⁷ And the peace of God, which surpasses all understanding, will guard your hearts and your minds in Christ Jesus.

**Hebrews 13:20-21 ESV**

[20] Now may the God of peace who brought again from the dead our Lord Jesus, the great shepherd of the sheep, by the blood of the eternal covenant, [21] equip you with everything good that you may do his will, working in us that which is pleasing in his sight, through Jesus Christ, to whom be glory forever and ever. Amen.

**John 16:31-33 ESV**

[31] Jesus answered them, "Do you now believe? [32] Behold, the hour is coming, indeed it has come, when you will be scattered, each to his own home, and will leave me alone. Yet I am not alone, for the Father is with me. [33] I have said these things to you, that in me you may have peace. In the world you will have tribulation. But take heart; I have overcome the world."

# Monday

**Read:** Luke 2:8-14

**Soap:** Luke 2:13-14

**Scripture** — Write out the **Scripture** passage for the day.

**Observations** — Write down 1 or 2 **observations** from the passage.

# Monday

*Applications* - Write down 1-2 **applications** from the passage.

*Pray* – Write out a prayer over what you learned from today's passage.

-Visit our website today for the corresponding blog post!-

# Tuesday

**Read:** John 14:25-27

**Soap:** John 14:27

**Scripture** – Write out the **Scripture** passage for the day.

**Observations** – Write down 1 or 2 **observations** from the passage.

# Tuesday

*Applications* - Write down 1-2 **applications** from the passage.

*Pray* — Write out a prayer over what you learned from today's passage.

# Wednesday

**Read:** Philippians 4:6-7

**Soap:** Philippians 4:7

**Scripture** — Write out the **Scripture** passage for the day.

**Observations** — Write down 1 or 2 **observations** from the passage.

# Wednesday

*Applications* - Write down 1-2 **applications** from the passage.

*Pray* — Write out a prayer over what you learned from today's passage.

-Visit our website today for the corresponding blog post!-

# Thursday

**Read:** Hebrews 13:20-21

**Soap:** Hebrews 13:20

**Scripture** – Write out the **Scripture** passage for the day.

**Observations** – Write down 1 or 2 **observations** from the passage.

# Thursday

*Applications* - Write down 1-2 **applications** from the passage.

*Pray* — Write out a prayer over what you learned from today's passage.

**Read:** John 16:31-33

**Soap:** John 16:33

**Scripture** — Write out the **Scripture** passage for the day.

**Observations** — Write down 1 or 2 **observations** from the passage.

# Friday

*Applications* - Write down 1-2 **applications** from the passage.

*Pray* — Write out a prayer over what you learned from today's passage.

-Visit our website today for the corresponding blog post!-

# *Reflection Questions*

## -PRINCE OF PEACE-

1. How has the peace of Jesus changed your life? How has it changed your intrapersonal relationship (self-concept, self-perception and future oriented expectations). How has it changed your interpersonal relationships (relationships with others)?

2. When you cannot appropriate God's abiding peace in your situation and/or circumstance, consider the following admonitions from God in Philippians 4:6-9 and apply these principles:

a) Praise God in all situations.

b) Pray and petition with thanksgiving over the concern.

c) Pursue obedience in your thought life: focus on what is true, noble, right, pure,

   lovely, admirable, excellent and praiseworthy.

d) Practical application of God's truth – put it into practice.

3. Reflect upon a time when God's peace supported and sustained you through a very difficult time. How did you know that God was guarding your heart and mind through that experience?

4. What does it mean to you to be reconciled to God? If the blood of Jesus satisfied divine justice, what is your fitting response to this ultimate sacrifice by Jesus Christ (Romans 12:1,2)?

5. Through Jesus Christ, the world is a conquered enemy. How can this knowledge bring peace in the midst of our personal trials and tribulations?

# My Response

## Week 4

**Week 4 Challenge** (Note: You can find this listed in our Monday blog post):

**Week 4 Memory Verse:**

This also comes from
the Lord of hosts;
he is wonderful in counsel
*and excellent in wisdom.*

ISAIAH 28:29

LoveGodGreatly.com

**Prayer focus for this week:** Your Church

| | Praying | Praise |
|---|---|---|
| Monday | | |
| Tuesday | | |
| Wednesday | | |
| Thursday | | |
| Friday | | |

# Week 4

## SCRIPTURE FOR THIS WEEK

**ISAIAH 28:29 ESV**

This also comes from the LORD of hosts;

  he is wonderful in counsel

  and excellent in wisdom.

**COLOSSIANS 2:1-3 ESV**

For I want you to know how great a struggle I have for you and for those at Laodicea and for all who have not seen me face to face, 2 that their hearts may be encouraged, being knit together in love, to reach all the riches of full assurance of understanding and the knowledge of God's mystery, which is Christ, 3 in whom are hidden all the treasures of wisdom and knowledge.

**JAMES 1:1-7 ESV**

James, a servant of God and of the Lord Jesus Christ,

To the twelve tribes in the Dispersion:

Greetings.

2 Count it all joy, my brothers, when you meet trials of various kinds, 3 for you know that the testing of your faith produces steadfastness. 4 And let steadfastness have its full effect, that you may be perfect and complete, lacking in nothing.

5 If any of you lacks wisdom, let him ask God, who gives generously to all without reproach, and it will be given him. 6 But let him ask in faith, with no doubting, for the one who doubts is like a wave of the sea that is driven and tossed by the wind. 7 For that person must not suppose that he will receive anything from the Lord;

## SCRIPTURE FOR THIS WEEK

**Revelation 7:11-12 ESV**

11 And all the angels were standing around the throne and around the elders and the four living creatures, and they fell on their faces before the throne and worshiped God, 12 saying, "Amen! Blessing and glory and wisdom and thanksgiving and honor and power and might be to our God forever and ever! Amen."

**Isaiah 9:6-7 ESV**

For to us a child is born,
  to us a son is given;
and the government shall be upon his shoulder,
  and his name shall be called
Wonderful Counselor, Mighty God,
  Everlasting Father, Prince of Peace.
7 Of the increase of his government and of peace
  there will be no end,
on the throne of David and over his kingdom,
  to establish it and to uphold it
with justice and with righteousness
  from this time forth and forevermore.
The zeal of the LORD of hosts will do this.

# Monday

**Read:** Isaiah 28:29

**Soap:** Isaiah 28:29

**Scripture** — Write out the **Scripture** passage for the day.

**Observations** — Write down 1 or 2 **observations** from the passage.

# Monday

## Applications - Write down 1-2 **applications** from the passage.

## Pray - Write out a prayer over what you learned from today's passage.

-Visit our website today for the corresponding blog post!-

# Tuesday

**Read:** Colossians 2:1-3

**Soap:** Colossians 2:3

**Scripture** — Write out the **Scripture** passage for the day.

**Observations** — Write down 1 or 2 **observations** from the passage.

# Tuesday

*Applications* - Write down 1-2 **applications** from the passage.

*Pray* — Write out a prayer over what you learned from today's passage.

# Wednesday

**Read:** James 1:1-7

**Soap:** James 1:5-6

**Scripture** — Write out the **Scripture** passage for the day.

**Observations** — Write down 1 or 2 **observations** from the passage.

# Wednesday

*Applications* - Write down 1-2 **applications** from the passage.

*Pray* - Write out a prayer over what you learned from today's passage.

-Visit our website today for the corresponding blog post!-

# Thursday

**Read:** Revelation 7:11-12

**Soap:** Revelation 7:11-12

**Scripture** — Write out the **Scripture** passage for the day.

**Observations** — Write down 1 or 2 **observations** from the passage.

# Thursday

*Applications* - Write down 1-2 **applications** from the passage.

*Pray* — Write out a prayer over what you learned from today's passage.

*Read:* Isaiah 9:6-7

*Soap:* Isaiah 9:6

*Scripture* — Write out the **Scripture** passage for the day.

*Observations* — Write down 1 or 2 **observations** from the passage.

# Friday

*Applications* - Write down 1-2 **applications** from the passage.

*Pray* — Write out a prayer over what you learned from today's passage.

-Visit our website today for the corresponding blog post!-

# Reflection Questions

## -WONDERFUL COUNSELOR-

1. God is able to use his Word to counsel us during life's journey. 2 Timothy 3:16 reads, "All Scripture is God-breathed and is useful for teaching, rebuking, correcting and training in righteousness." Considering these four areas, when and how did God last teach, rebuke, correct and train you in righteousness?

2. It is not uncommon to seek out counsel from trusted family, friends or counselors prior to seeking God's wisdom and knowledge. During the next week, challenge yourself to share your concerns with God through prayer and seek His counsel through His Word before you call upon anyone else.

3. What makes you feel as though God is not hearing your prayers? Remember, delayed prayers are not God's denial.

4. What are ways that you personally bless, glorify and give thanksgiving to God throughout the week?

5. When in your life did you experience God as your Wonderful Counselor, your Mighty God, your Everlasting Father and your Prince of Peace?

# My Response

-WEEK 4-

**Week 5 Challenge** (Note: You can find this listed in our Monday blog post):

**Week 5 Memory Verse:**

*Fear not,*
for I am with you;
be not dismayed,
for I am your God;
*I will strengthen you,*
I will help you,
I will uphold you
with my righteous right hand.

ISAIAH 41:10

LoveGodGreatly.com

**Prayer focus for this week:** Missionaries

| | Praying | Praise |
|---|---|---|
| *Monday* | | |
| *Tuesday* | | |
| *Wednesday* | | |
| *Thursday* | | |
| *Friday* | | |

**Matthew 1:18-23 ESV**

18 Now the birth of Jesus Christ took place in this way. When his mother Mary had been betrothed to Joseph, before they came together she was found to be with child from the Holy Spirit. 19 And her husband Joseph, being a just man and unwilling to put her to shame, resolved to divorce her quietly. 20 But as he considered these things, behold, an angel of the Lord appeared to him in a dream, saying, "Joseph, son of David, do not fear to take Mary as your wife, for that which is conceived in her is from the Holy Spirit. 21 She will bear a son, and you shall call his name Jesus, for he will save his people from their sins." 22 All this took place to fulfill what the Lord had spoken by the prophet:

23 "Behold, the virgin shall conceive and bear a son,
  and they shall call his name Immanuel"


**Isaiah 41:10 ESV**

fear not, for I am with you;
  be not dismayed, for I am your God;
I will strengthen you, I will help you,
  I will uphold you with my righteous right hand.


**Matthew 28:16-20 ESV**

16 Now the eleven disciples went to Galilee, to the mountain to which Jesus had directed them. 17 And when they saw him they worshiped him, but some doubted. 18 And Jesus came and said to them, "All authority in heaven and on earth has been given to me. 19 Go therefore and make disciples of all nations, baptizing them in the name of the Father and of the Son and of the Holy Spirit, 20 teaching them to observe all that I have commanded you. And behold, I am with you always, to the end of the age."

**Jeremiah 23:23-24 ESV**

23 "Am I a God at hand, declares the LORD, and not a God far away? 24 Can a man hide himself in secret places so that I cannot see him? declares the LORD. Do I not fill heaven and earth? declares the LORD.

**Galatians 2:20 ESV**

20 I have been crucified with Christ. It is no longer I who live, but Christ who lives in me. And the life I now live in the flesh I live by faith in the Son of God, who loved me and gave himself for me.

# Monday

**Read:** Matthew 1:18-23

**Soap:** Matthew 1:23

**Scripture** — Write out the **Scripture** passage for the day.

**Observations** — Write down 1 or 2 **observations** from the passage.

# Monday

**Applications** - Write down 1-2 **applications** from the passage.

**Pray** - Write out a prayer over what you learned from today's passage.

-Visit our website today for the corresponding blog post!-

# Tuesday

*Read:* Isaiah 41:10

*Soap:* Isaiah 41:10

*Scripture* — Write out the **Scripture** passage for the day.

*Observations* — Write down 1 or 2 **observations** from the passage.

# Tuesday

*Applications* - Write down 1-2 **applications** from the passage.

*Pray* — Write out a prayer over what you learned from today's passage.

# Wednesday

**Read:** Matthew 28:16-20

**Soap:** Matthew 28:20

**Scripture** — Write out the **Scripture** passage for the day.

**Observations** — Write down 1 or 2 **observations** from the passage.

# Wednesday

*Applications* - Write down 1-2 **applications** from the passage.

*Pray* — Write out a prayer over what you learned from today's passage.

-Visit our website today for the corresponding blog post!-

# Thursday

**Read:** Jeremiah 23:23-24

**Soap:** Jeremiah 23:23-24

**Scripture** – Write out the **Scripture** passage for the day.

**Observations** – Write down 1 or 2 **observations** from the passage.

# Thursday

*Applications* - Write down 1-2 **applications** from the passage.

*Pray* — Write out a prayer over what you learned from today's passage.

**Read:** Galatians 2:20

**Soap:** Galatians 2:20

**Scripture** — Write out the **Scripture** passage for the day.

**Observations** — Write down 1 or 2 **observations** from the passage.

# Friday

*Applications* - Write down 1-2 **applications** from the passage.

*Pray* — Write out a prayer over what you learned from today's passage.

-Visit our website today for the corresponding blog post!-

# Reflection Questions

## -EMMANUEL-

1. Since Jesus' birth was prophesied more than 700 years earlier in Isaiah 7:14, how does this demonstration of God's infinite knowledge and power impact your daily interactions with God?

2. Think of a time when God intervened on your behalf and exhibited his love, care, help and/or support to you during a very crucial time in your life. Describe how it felt to be loved so personally by your heavenly Father.

3. List several reasons why our obedience to God is important.

4. Why can the omniscience of God give you peace in this life and joy in the life to come? What passages of Scripture speak to God's omniscience?

5. We are continually surrendering areas of our life to Jesus. What parts of your life are still under your control? What would it take for you to yield these areas over to Jesus?

# My Response

-WEEK 5-

**Week 6 Challenge** (Note: You can find this listed in our Monday blog post):

**Week 6 Memory Verse:**

"For God so loved the world,
that he gave his only Son,
that whoever believes in him
should not perish
but have eternal life.

JOHN 3:16

LoveGodGreatly.com

**Prayer focus for this week:** Spend time thanking God for how He is working in your life.

| | Praying | Praise |
|---|---|---|
| Monday | | |
| Tuesday | | |
| Wednesday | | |
| Thursday | | |
| Friday | | |

**MATTHEW 1:20-22 ESV**

But as he considered these things, behold, an angel of the Lord appeared to him in a dream, saying, "Joseph, son of David, do not fear to take Mary as your wife, for that which is conceived in her is from the Holy Spirit. [21] She will bear a son, and you shall call his name Jesus, for he will save his people from their sins." [22] All this took place to fulfill what the Lord had spoken by the prophet:

**MARK 2:16-17 ESV**

[16] And the scribes of the Pharisees, when they saw that he was eating with sinners and tax collectors, said to his disciples, "Why does he eat with tax collectors and sinners?"[17] And when Jesus heard it, he said to them, "Those who are well have no need of a physician, but those who are sick. I came not to call the righteous, but sinners."

**1 TIMOTHY 1:15-17 ESV**

[15] The saying is trustworthy and deserving of full acceptance, that Christ Jesus came into the world to save sinners, of whom I am the foremost. [16] But I received mercy for this reason, that in me, as the foremost, Jesus Christ might display his perfect patience as an example to those who were to believe in him for eternal life. [17] To the King of the ages immortal, invisible, the only God, be honor and glory forever and ever. Amen.

**ISAIAH 53:3-7 ESV**

He was despised and rejected by men;
 a man of sorrows, and acquainted with grief;
and as one from whom men hide their faces
 he was despised, and we esteemed him not.

## SCRIPTURE FOR THIS WEEK

4 Surely he has borne our grief

  and carried our sorrows;

yet we esteemed him stricken,

  smitten by God, and afflicted.

5 But he was pierced for our transgressions;

  he was crushed for our iniquities;

upon him was the chastisement that brought us peace,

  and with his wounds we are healed.

6 All we like sheep have gone astray;

  we have turned—every one—to his own way;

and the LORD has laid on him

  the iniquity of us all.

7 He was oppressed, and he was afflicted,

  yet he opened not his mouth;

like a lamb that is led to the slaughter,

  and like a sheep that before its shearers is silent,

  so he opened not his mouth.

**John 3:16-18 ESV**

16 "For God so loved the world, that he gave his only Son, that whoever believes in him should not perish but have eternal life. 17 For God did not send his Son into the world to condemn the world, but in order that the world might be saved through him. 18 Whoever believes in him is not condemned, but whoever does not believe is condemned already, because he has not believed in the name of the only Son of God.

# Monday

**Read:** Matthew 1:20-22

**Soap:** Matthew 1:21

**Scripture** — Write out the **Scripture** passage for the day.

**Observations** — Write down 1 or 2 **observations** from the passage.

# Monday

*Applications* - Write down 1-2 **applications** from the passage.

*Pray* – Write out a prayer over what you learned from today's passage.

-Visit our website today for the corresponding blog post!-

# Tuesday

**Read:** Mark 2:16-17

**Soap:** Mark 2:17

**Scripture** — Write out the **Scripture** passage for the day.

**Observations** — Write down 1 or 2 **observations** from the passage.

# Tuesday

*Applications* - Write down 1-2 **applications** from the passage.

*Pray* — Write out a prayer over what you learned from today's passage.

# Wednesday

**Read:** 1 Timothy 1:15-17

**Soap:** 1 Timothy 1:15

**Scripture** — Write out the **Scripture** passage for the day.

**Observations** — Write down 1 or 2 **observations** from the passage.

# Wednesday

*Applications*- Write down 1-2 **applications** from the passage.

*Pray*- Write out a prayer over what you learned from today's passage.

-Visit our website today for the corresponding blog post!-

# Thursday

**Read:** Isaiah 53:3-7

**Soap:** Isaiah 53:6

**Scripture** — Write out the **Scripture** passage for the day.

**Observations** — Write down 1 or 2 **observations** from the passage.

# Thursday

*Applications* - Write down 1-2 **applications** from the passage.

*Pray* — Write out a prayer over what you learned from today's passage.

# Friday

**Read:** John 3:16-18

**Soap:** John 3:16

**Scripture** — Write out the **Scripture** passage for the day.

**Observations** — Write down 1 or 2 **observations** from the passage.

# Friday

*Applications* - Write down 1-2 **applications** from the passage.

*Pray* — Write out a prayer over what you learned from today's passage.

-Visit our website today for the corresponding blog post!-

# Reflection Questions

## -JESUS-

1. What is required for you to be forgiven from your sins?

2. Consider who in your life does not feel their need for a Savior. Pray for these individuals to see their need.

3. What sin in your own life do you find difficult to believe Jesus has forgiven?

4. Think about the sins you struggle with on a daily basis. Praise the Lord that He died for all of your sins - past, present and future.

5. Praise God today that God so loved you that if you were the only person in the world he would have died to ensure your eternal future.

# My Response

-WEEK 6-

Made in the USA
Lexington, KY
05 October 2016